A-Z of Baby Bo

Choosing a Name Fo

CU00842181

Erica Harvey

Erica Harvey

Erica Harvey

CHAPTER LISTING

Erica Harvey

A-Z of Baby Boy Names

INTRODUCTION

Choosing a name for your baby is one of the most important and daunting aspects of being a parent. It can leave you clueless and indecisive at the best of times. There are just so many names out there and most parents (maybe even you) ask themselves all sorts of questions: should we go for a more traditional name or a popular one? Should we name our child after our heritage or the culture they grew up around? Should we give the child a masculine name or a feminine one? And so on and so forth. What's difficult about the naming process is that as a parent, you can't know for sure how well the name will suit the baby that you are raising.

The reality is, there is no right answer to the question. It sounds basic but it really is down to you as the baby's parent i.e *you*. You don't know anything about the baby's personality, future career, likes and dislikes so choosing a name might simply seem like picking out of a hat at random.

Don't worry, this guide has you covered. Not only will you get an extensive A-Z of male and female names, but also, the meanings are provided with each so you won't feel as though you're naming the baby based solely on the sound of the name alone. You might be wondering how to choose from such a long list?

There are steps that can help you decide. They are as follows:

1. Choose 3 letters that you like in particular. You can determine these letters based on which ones had the most names that hit your ear right or based on which ones had the most relevant meaning for what you would picture your son to be like.

2. Choose 5 names from each letter and write them in big capitals on a piece of paper.

3. Say each one out loud, one at a time.

4. Narrow down from 5 names per letter to 2. You should now have 6 names.

5. Now it's time for the hard part. You have to narrow it down even further to three names based on your own opinion (and that of your partner if relevant).

6. Once you have two final names, write them on sticky notes or on pieces of paper. Place them around your house for a week in areas that you frequent quite regularly e.g. kitchen, bathroom etc. Allow yourself to get used to these names. After a while, you'll realise subconsciously which one you prefer and which sounds right.

Selecting the perfect name can be hard. Consider the following when choosing a name.

1. Characteristics of a name. Do phrases like 'God with us' (Emanuel) resonate with you or are you more of a quick-fire one word definition sort of person like 'snow' (Yuki) or 'sky' (Kalani)?

2. Choosing the name of a relative/ ancestor. It is common and actually a very fitting family tribute to name your son after your grandfather/mother/father/ great grandfather/ aunt/ uncle who meant a lot to you for personal sentimental reasons. Perhaps consider this when choosing a name and if you go down this route, maybe change the spelling and make it original.

Some psychologists believe that there are inherent differences in the way we choose boys' names compared with how girls' names are chosen. This is in the way that the name affects or represent that child.

In essence, parents typically name boys after traits which they perceive would suit their ideal son (usually a lot of masculinity) whereas girls names are traditionally chosen based on delicacy and femininity. While this might sound old-fashioned, many cultures still follow this.

By all means follow this if it works for you but you have to choose a good name based on your own inclinations.

Consider:

What sounds right?

What definition suits you, your culture, your beliefs. Is the name going to bring unwanted attention?

On the point of unwanted attention, it must be made

very clear that you should not choose a name which is either illegal or suggestive of something detrimental or socially taboo. For example, steer clear of names like:

- Satan
- Adolf
- Lucifer (unless it's an abbreviated form such as 'Luci')
- Evil

Naming your child is such a personal affair. You will come to realise that you not only bond with the individual that you have brought into the world but also, you'll connect with their name.

When we are assigned a name, so much comes with it. We don't realise it but when someone introduces themselves to us, we subconsciously take on that name and identify many character traits based on it alone. A name tells us about where a person comes from, their social class, heritage and so many other factors.

As a parent, you should be aware of this and choose a name which your heart connects with. A name that states clearly, "this is my son/daughter". It might take you a while to find out what that name is, but when you do, it's a rewarding experience.

Another tip I'd like to give is that it's okay to be unsure. You shouldn't have one eureka moment of certainty. You might, but it's not unusual to go through phases until one or two names stick after a while and then you can narrow it down from there.

NAMES FOR HIM

Aaden

Fire, Boy of Fire

Aaron

Exalted by God/ Chosen Brother

Abdiel

Servant of God/ Elected

Abel

Breath of Life

Abner

The Father is of the Light

Abraham

Father of the the Nations

Abram

Mighty Father

Ace

Of Highest Rank

Achilles

Tribe's Grief

Adam

Man/ Man of clay/ First man/ New Creation/ Father's Image

Aden

Little Fire

Adler

Eagle

Adolfo

Noble Wolf

Adonis

My Lord

Adriel

God's Followers

Adrian/Adrien/ Adrienn/ Adriaan

Man of Hadria

Aedan

boy Fire, little fire

Agustin/Augustine

Venerated/ Respected

Aidan/Aiden/Aidyn

Fire

Alan

Rock

Albert

Noble

Alberto

Noble

Alden

Friend

Aldo

Old/Wise

Alec/Alex/Alexander/Alexis

boy Defending men

Alejandro

Defender of all Men

Alessandro

Defender of all Men

Alfred

Counsel

Alfredo

Counsel

Ali

Sublime/Elegant/Majestic

Alijah

My God is the Lord/ My God is the One

Alistair

Sacred Keeper of Men

Allan

Stone

Alonso

Prepared

Alton

Old Town

Alvaro

Army

Alvin

Friend

Amare

Handsome/ Majestic

Amari

Noble

Amarion

Thriving/ Succeeding/ Flourishing

Amauri

Hard Worker

Amir

Prince (Arabic/Urdu) / Small Fruit (Aramaic) / Sheriff (Persian) / Leader (Turkish)

Ammon

The One Who is Hidden

Amos

Carrier/ Burden Bringer (from the Hebrew Prophet *Amos*)

Anakin

Defender of Strength

Anas

Friendly

Anders

Manly

Anderson

Son of Anders/Andrew

Andre

Man/ Boy

Angel

Messenger/ God's Companion/ Those from Above (in Gnosticism)

Angelo

Small Messenger

Angus

With Strength

Anish

Supreme

Anson

Son of Agnes/Annis/ Anas

Anthony

Flower

Antoine

Flower

Anton

Plant of Earth

Antonio

Garden

Antwan

Plant of Earth

Apollo

Messenger

Archer

Practicer of Archery

Archie

Practicer of Archery (nickname).

Ares

Destroyer

Ari

Lion

Arlo

Mountain/Hill/Valley

Arman

Aspiration/Dream/Goal/Eventuality

Armando

Man of the Army

Armani

Army

Arnav

Ocean/Sea/Flowing Waters

Arnold

Power of the Eagle/Eagle's Flight

Austin

Venerated

Aven

Counsel.

Avery

Counsel

Avi

Father of Mine

Ayaan

Flight/Motion

Azael

Made of God

Azariah

God has Helped/Saved

Baron

Young Warrior

Barrett

Deceptive

Barry

Fair Haired

Baylor

Sealer of Barrels

Beau

Handsome (French origin)

Beckett

Brook

Beckham

a Settlement

Ben

Blessed is He

Benedict

Blessed Man

Benicio

Blessed Man

Benito

Blessed

Benjamin

Son of the Right Hand

Bennett

Blessed Boy

Benny

Abbreviated form of Benedict

Benson

Son of Benedict

Bentley

Meadow

Benton

Town of Benson

Bernard

Brave/Masculine/Strong

Bernardo

Brave

Bilal

Thirst Quencher

Billy

The Desired

Bishop

Overseer/ Head of the Church

Blaine

Yellow

Blake

Darkness/Night

Blaze

Stammer

Bo

Handsome (Alternative spelling of 'Beau')

Bobby

Shortened form of 'Robert'

Braydon

Descendent of Bradán

Braylen

Descendant of Bradán

Brendan

Prince

Brenden

Prince

Brendon

Prince

Bronx

Land of Bronze/Bronck's Land

Brooks

Of a Brook

Bruce

Boy From Brix

Bruno

Brown

Bryan

Boy From Brionne

Bryant

High/Powerful

Bryce

Speckled

Brycen

Son of Brice

Bryson

Son of Brice

Cade

Swollen/Round/Rotund

Caden

Son of Cadán

Cael

Thin/Slender/Long

Caiden

Son of Cadán

Cain

Spear/Older Brother

Cal

Abbreviated form of any name beginning with 'Cal'.

Cale

Oneness

Caleb

Dog/Loyal

Callum

Dove/Holy Bird

Calvin

Bald

Camari

Crooked

Camden

Enclosed valley/Winding valley

Cameron

Crooked nose

Camilo

Servant of God's Temple

Camren

Crooked nose

Canaan

Merchant

Cannon

Canon

Canyon

Canyon

Carl

Freed from Slavery

Carlo/Carlos

Free man

Carlton

Settlement of free men

Carmelo

Orchard/Beautiful Garden

Carmine

Garden

Carson

He who is with Christ

Carsten

Christian Man (Scottish Origin)

Carter

He who transports materials

Carver

Sculptor of Wood

Case

Of a Situation

Casen

Variation of Case

Casey

Descendant of Cathasach

Cash

Money

Cason

House

Cassius

He who is vain/empty

Cayden

Son of Cadán

Cecil

Blinded

Cedric

Gift/Splendour/Wonderment

Cesar

He who is hairy

Chase/Chace/Chasse/Chacce/Chayce/Chaise/Chaice

To hunt/pounce

please note that on names with variations, choose the one that looks best to you.

Chad

Battle/Confrontation

Chaim

Life/Alive

Chance

Luck/fortune

Chandler

Candle Vendor/He who sells candles

Channing

Son of Cana/Man from Canaan

Charles

Free man

Charlie

Free man

Chester

Strong Camp/community

Chevy/Chevalier/Chev

Knight

Chris/Christian

a Christian

Christopher

He who bears Christ

Cian

Ancient

Clarence

Belonging to Clare

Clark

Cleric/Biblical scholar

Clay

Clay/Sculptor of Clay

Clayton

a Clay Area/Turf

Clifford

The Ford by a Cliff

Clifton

Settlement by a Cliff

Clint/Clinton

Settlement of a Summit

Clyde

He who is of Powerful Hearing

Coby

Supplanter/Importer of Goods

Cody

Son of Otto

Coen

Holy Priest of God

Cohen

Priest

Colby

Coal

Cole

Coal/Darkness

Coleman

Coal Worker/Mine Worker

Colin

Victory of the people

Collin

Victory of the people

Colson/Colsson/Collson/Collsson

Son of Nicholas

Colt

Young male horse

Colten

Cola's town

Colton

Cola's town

Conner

Lover of hounds

Connor

Lover of hounds

Conrad

Experienced

Constantine

Steadfast/Consistent

Cooper

Maker of barrels

Corbin

Raven/Crow

Cordell

Cord Maker

Corey

Hollow/Ditch

Cormac

Son of a Charioteer

Dakota

Friend

Dale

Valley Dweller

Dallas

Dwelling in the Meadow

Dalton

Town in the valley

Damarion

Tamed Man

Damian/Damien/Damion/Damon

to Tame

Daniel/Dan

God is my judge

Dane

Valley

Dangelo

Descendant of Angelo

Danny

God is my judge

Dante

Enduring

Darian

Poet/Gift

Dariel

Man of Airelle

Darien

Gift

Dario

Goodness

Davian

Beloved Man

David

Beloved by God

Davis

Son of David

Dawson

Son of David

Dax

boy From Dax

Daxton

Man From Dax

Dayton

Dairy town

Deacon

A deacon

Dean

Valley

Deangelo

Messenger

Declan

Man of Prayer

Deegan

Black-haired (Gaelic origin)

Demarco

Son of Marco

Demarcus

Son of Marcus

Demari

Son of Mary

Demario

Calf/ Son of Mario

Demetrius

Earth Mother

Dennis

Son Of Zeus

Denver

Crossing

Denzel

Fort

Deon

Son Of Zeus

Deonte

Boy

Derek

Ruler of the people

Derick

Ruler of the people

Derrick

boy Ruler of the people

Deshawn

Son of Shawn/Sunlight

Desmond

Man from south Munster

Destin

boy The meaning of Destin is unknown...

Dev

God

Devan

Dark

Deven

Dark

Devin

Dark

Devon

Worshippers of the Pagan God Dumnōnos

Devonte

Men of Devon

Devyn

Of Darkness

Dexter

Cloth Dryer

Dhruv

Constant

Diego

Supplanter/Importer of Goods

Diesel

Mineral/Oil

Dillon

High Tide/Tidal Wave

Dimitri

Follower of Demeter

Dominic

Of the Lord

Don

Abbreviated form of any name starting with 'Don'.

Donald

Ruler of the World

Donavan

Descendant of Donndubhán

Donnell

Ruler of the world

Donovan

Descendant of Donndubhán

Donte

Enduring/Stamina

Drake

Dragon

Draven

Pagan God

Drew

Manly

Duke

Leader

Duncan

Brown Warrior

Dustin

Dusty

Dwayne

Descendant of Dubhán

Dwight

Of Zeus

Dylan

Tide

Eamon

Rich

Ean

God is Gracious

Earl

Warrior

Easton

Settlement located by a River

Eben

Stone of Help

Eddie

Abbreviated form of 'Edward'.

Eden

Pleasure/Appeasement/Appealing Place

Eder

Beauty

Edgar

Spearman

Edison

Blessed Guard

Edmund

Rich Protector

Edson

Guard

Eduardo

Blessed Guard

Edward

Blessed Guard

Edwin

Friend

Efrain

Twice Fruitful

Efren

Twice Fruitful

Elam

Hidden One

Elan

Tree

Eleazar

God has helped me

Eli

Height

Elian

My God is the Lord

Elias

My God is the Lord

Eliel

The Lord is my God

Eliezer

My Lord is help

Elijah

My God is the Lord

Eliseo

My God is helpful

Elisha

both My God is help

Eliyahu

My God is the Lord

Elliot

My God is the Lord

Elliott

My God is the Lord

Ellis

My God is the Lord

Elmer

Famous

Elton

Ella's town

Elvin

Friend of the Elves

Emanuel

God is with us

Emerson

Home

Emery

Labour

Emil

Rival

Emiliano

Work

Emmett

Universal

Ender

Very Rare

Enoch

Dedicated to God

Enrique

Ruler of the Homeland

Ephraim

Fruitful/ Fertile

Eric

Forever the Ruler

Ernest

Serious

Ernesto

Serious

Ervin

Friend of the Army

Erwin

Friend of the Army

Eshan

Ruler

Esteban

King's Crown

Ethan

Enduring/Stable/Solid/Powerful

Ethen

Lasting

Eugene

Well-born/ Healthy child

Evan

God is gracious

Ever

Beyond

Everardo

As a Wild Boar

Everett

Brave Boar

Ewan

Yew Tree

Ezekiel

God will give me strength (from the Hebrew prophet '*Ezekiel*').

Ezra

Helpful

Fabian

Bean/Root

Federico

Peaceful ruler

Felipe

Horse's Friend

Felix

Lucky

Fidel

Faithful

Finley

White Warrior

Finn

Fair/White

Finnegan

Descendent of Fionnagán

Finnian

Fair

Fisher

Fisherman/ Fish Monger

Flavio

Golden

Fletcher

Arrow Maker

Floyd

Grey

Flynn

Descendent of Flann

Ford

River Crossing

Forrest

Woods

Foster

Forest keeper

Fox

Fox

Francesco

Frenchman

Francis

Frenchman

Francisco

Frenchman

Franco

Frenchman

Frank

Pertaining to France

Frankie

Frenchman

Franklin

Landholder

Fred

Peaceful ruler

Freddy

Peaceful ruler

Frederick

Peaceful ruler

Gabriel

God is my strength

Gaël

Giving

Gage

Measurer/ Surveyor

Garret

Brave Spear

Garrison

Fortification

Gary

Spear

Geoffrey

Stranger

George

Farmer

Gerald

The Spear's rule

Gerard

Brave spear

German

Army man

Gerson

Stranger

Gian

God is gracious

Gianni

God is kind

Gibson

Son of Gilbert

Gideon

God's Mighty Warrior

Gilbert

an Oath/Pledge

Glenn

Valley

Gonzalo

War

Gordon

Spacious Fort/ Castle

Grady

Noble

Graham

Homestead

Grant

Big/ Huge/ Large

Grayden

Grey Ditch

Grayson

Son of Gray

Gregory

Watchman

Griffin

Lord/ Prince of All

Guillermo

Desire

Gunnar

Warrior

Guy

Guider

Haden

Hay valley

Hagen

Enclosure

Haiden

Hay valley

Hank

Home ruler

Harlan

Land of hares

Harlem

The Name of a Town

Harley

Clearing in a Hare Den

Harold

Army Leader

Harris ✓

Son of Harry

Harrison ✓

Son of Harry

Harry

Army leader

Harvey

Worthy of Battle

Hassan

Beautiful Boy

Haven

Safety

Heath

He who dwells on a Heath

Hector

Fast

Hendrix

Home ruler

Herbert

Bright army

Heriberto

Bright army

Herman

Army man

Hernan

Brave Journey

Hezekiah

He who God Strengthens

Hiram

Brother who is Exalted

Holden

Deep valley

Hollis

Holly trees

Holt

One who lives near a wood

Houston

Village

Howard

Brave Heart

Hoyt

Wooden Stick

Hudson

Son of Hugh

Hugh

Heart

Hugo

Heart/ Mind

Humberto

The Famous warrior

Hunter

One who hunts

Ian

God is gracious

Ibrahim

Father of the multitude

Ignacio

Fire/ Ignition

Iker

Visitation/ He who God Visits

Ilan

Tree

Ira

Watchful

Irvin

Green Water

Isaac

He who Laughs

Isael

He who God contends with

Isai

He who Is

Isaiah

God is salvation

Isaias

He who God saves

Ishaan

Ruler

Isidro

Gift of Isis

Ismael

God will hear you

Israel

God contended

Issac

boy He laughs

Jabari

Bringer of comfort

Jace

Healer

Jack

God is gracious

Jackson

Son of Jack

Jacob

Held by the heel

Jad

Benevolent

Jadiel

God is my Fortune

Jadon

God will judge

Jael

Mountain Goat

Jagger

Peddler

Jair

He will shine

Jairo

He shines

Jake

God is gracious

Jamal

Beauty

James

Held by the heel

Jameson

Son of James

Jamil

Beauty

Jared

Descent

Jaren

He who will rejoice

Jaron

He who will rejoice

Jarrett

Brave spear

Jarvis

Spear Wielder

Jase

Healer

Jason

Healer

Jasper

Treasure bearer

Javen

Beginning

Javier

New House

Jedidiah

Beloved of Yahweh (God)

Jeff

Territory

Jefferson

Son of Jeffrey

Jelani

Strong

Jensen

Son of Jens

Jeremiah

God has raised

Jeremy

God has raised

Jericho

The Israeli town Jericho

Jermaine

Brother

Jesiah

God's Gift

Jesus/ Yeshua/ Jeshuah

God is Salvation

Jett

Airplane

Jimmy

Held by the heel

Joaquin

Raised by God

Joe

God Increases

Joel

God is the True Lord

Joey

He who increases

Johan

God is gracious

John

God is full of Grace

Johnathan

He who is Given by God

Jonah

Dove/ God's Messenger

Jonathan

Given by God

Jordan

Descend/ Flow down

Jordy

Flowing down

Jorge

Farmer

José

God increases

Joseph

God increases

Josh

God is salvation

Joshua

God is salvation

Josiah

God saves

Josue

God saves

Jovan

God is gracious

Jovani

God is gracious

Juan

God is gracious

Juancarlos

Juan and Carlos combination

Judah

Praised by God

Jude

Gratitude of God

Judson

Son of Jordan

Juelz

Bearded Young Man

Julian

Bearded Young Man

Junior

A boy named after his father

Justice

Fairness

Justin

Just/ Equal

Kade

Round

Kaden

Son of Cadán

Kadin

Son of Cadán

Kadyn

Son of Cadán

Kaeden

Son of Cadán

Kael

Slender

Kage

Cage

Kai

Sea

Kain

Spear/ Pierce

Kainoa

He who is Named

Kalani

The Sky

Kaleb

Dog/ Canine

Kalel

Vessel of God

Kamal

Perfection

Kamar

Moon

Kamari

Enemy of desire

Kareem

Generous

Karl

Free Man

Karsten

a Follower of Christ

Karter

Cart Carrier

Karthik

Bestower of happiness

Kayden

Battle

Kayson

House

Keagan

Descendent of Aodhagán

Keanu

The cool air

Keaton

Town of sheds

Keegan

Descendent of Aodhagán

Keelan

Slender

Keenan

Descendent of Cathán

Keion

Leader

Keith

Woodland

Kelby

Child's town

Kellan

Slender

Keller

Companion

Kelton

Man from Kirkcudbrightshire

Kelvin

The river Clyde

Ken

Fireborn

Lamar

Ocean/ Sea

Lamont

Lawyer

Lance

Land

Landen

Ridge/ Long hill

Landin

Hill

Landry

Master of My Land

Langston

Long/Big Stone

Laron

Variant of Darren.

Larry

Man from Laurentum

Lars

Man from Laurentum

Latrell

Otter

Lawrence

Man from Laurentum

Lawson

Son of Laurence

Layne

Path/Lane/Pathway

Layton

Garden Settlement

Lazaro

God has helped me

Lazarus

God has helped me

Leandro

Lion Man

Lebron

Basket

Ledger

Book

Lee

Meadow

Legend

Popular myth

Leif

Heir to the Thrown

Leighton

Settlement

Leland

Fallow land

Leo/ Leon

Lion

Leonard

Brave Lion

Leonardo

Brave lion

Leonel

Lion

Leroy

The king

Lester

From the city of Leicester

Levi

Attached/ Combined

Lewis

Famous warrior

Liam

Deep Desire

Lincoln

Pool of Water/ Lake/ River

Linus

Flax

Lionel

Lion

Lisandro

Release the Man

Lloyd

Grey

Lochlan

Loch Lands

Logan

Hollow

London

Capital City of England

Lonnie

Ready for Battle

Lorenzo

Man from Laurentum

Louis

Famous warrior

Luca

From Luciana

Lucas

From Lucania

Lucian

Light

Lucio

Light

Lucius

Light

Luke

From Lucania

Luther

Army of people

Lyle

Island

Lyndon

Of the lime tree

Lyric

Words to a song

Mac

Son of a Father

Mack

Greatness

Madden

Of a Hound

Maddox

Son of Madoc

Magnus

He who is Great

Makai

Towards the sea

Malachi

My angel

Malakai

My messenger

Malaki

My angel

Malcolm

Dove

Malik

King

Manny

God is with us

Manuel

God is with us

Marc

Of the Roman god Mars

Marcel

Of the Roman god Mars

Marcelino

Little Marcus

Mario

From the sea

Marion

Bitter sea

Marley

Pleasant woods

Marlon

Variation of Marley

Marshall

Horse servant

Marshawn

God is gracious

Mason

Stoneworker

Massimo

Greatest

Mateo

Gift of God

Mathew

Gift of God

Mathias

Gift of God

Matias

Gift of God

Matteo

Gift of God

Matthew

Gift of God

Matthias

Gift of God

Maurice

Dark skin

Mauricio

Dark skin

Mauro

Dark skinned

Maverick

Independent

Max

Great One

Maxim

Greatest

Maximilian

Greatest

Maximiliano

Greatest

Maximo

Greatest

Maximus

Greatest

Maxwell

Mack's stream

McCoy

Son of Lewis

McKay

Son of Aodh

Meir

He who shines

Mekhi

Who is like God

Melvin

Infertile settlement

Menachem

One who gives comfort

Mendel

One who gives comfort

Merrick

Power

Messiah

Anointed by Yahweh (God)

Micah

Who is like God

Micaiah

Who is like God

Michael

Who is like God

Micheal

Who is like God

Mickey

Who is like God

Miguel

Who is like God

Miguelangel

Combination of Miguel and Angel

Mike

Who is like God

Milan

Gracious

Miles

Soldier

Miller

Grain Grinder

Morgan

Born of the sea

Morris

Dark-skinned

Moses

Son

Moshe

Son

Muhammad

Worthy of praise

Murphy

Descendant of Murchadh

Musa

Saved from the water

Mustafa

One who is chosen

Myles

Soldier

Myron

Myrrh

Nash

At the ash tree

Nasir

Helper

Nate

God has given

Nathan/ Nathanial

He has given

Nehemiah

Comforted by god

Neil

Champion

Nelson

Son of Neil

Nestor

Homecoming

Nevin

Little saint

Nicholas

Victory of the people

Nick

Victory of the people

Nickolas

Victory of the people

Nico

Victory of the people

Nicolas

Victory of the people

Nigel

Champion/ Passionate

Nikhil

Entire

Nikita

Victory

Niko

Victory of the people

Nikolai

Victory of the people

Nixon

Son of Nicholas

Noah

Comfort/ Rest

Noe

Rest

Noël

Christmas

Nolan

Descended from Nuallán

Norman

Man from the north

Oakley

From the oak meadow

Obed

Worshipper

Ocean

Sea

Octavio

Eighth

Odin

Rage

Oliver

Army

Omar

He who thrives

Orlando

Famous land

Oscar

Deer lover

Osiel

My power is God

Osiris

Egyptian God of the dead

Osman

Baby bird

Osmar

Wonderful

Osvaldo

God's rule

Oswaldo

God's rule

Otis

Wealth

Otto

Wealth/ Fortune

Owen

Born from the yew

Pablo

Humble

Palmer

Pilgram

Parker

Gamekeeper

Patricio

Noble

Patrick

Nobleman

Patton

Nobleman

Paul

Humble

Paulo

Humble

Pavel

Humble

Paxton

Pœcc's town

Pearce

Stone

Pedro

Stone

Peter

Stone

Peyton

Pœga's town

Philip

Friend of horses

Phoenix

Phoenix

Pierce

Stone

Pierre

Stone

Pierson

Stone

Porter

Doorkeeper

Preston

Town for priests

Prince

Son of the royal family

Quade

Ruler of the army

Quadir

He who is Able

Quentin

Fifth

Quincy

Fifth

Quinlan

Descendant of Caoinlean

Quinn

Chief

Quran

The sacred writing of Islam.

Rafael

God has healed

Raiden

Thunder and lightning

Raleigh

Red wood

Ralph

Wolf council

Ramiro

Advice

Ramón

Advice

Ramsey

Island of wild garlic

Randall

Edge of a shield

Randy

Edge of a shield

Raphael

God has healed

Rashad

Wisdom

Raúl

Wolf council

Ray

Advice

Rayan

Sweet Basil

Raymond

Advice

Reece

Enthusiasm

Reed

Ginger Haired

Reggie

Advice

Reginald

Advice

Reid

Red

Remington

Boundary

Rémy

Oarsman

René

Reborn

Reuben

Behold My Son

Rex

King

Rey

King

Reynaldo

Advice

Rhett

Advice

Rhys

Enthusiasm

Rían

Little king

Ricardo

Ruler of All

Richard

Power/ Rule

Rick

Power

Ridge

Ridge

Riley

Clearing

Rio

Jasmine village

Rishi

Seer

River

a River

Roan

Raven Bird

Robert

Bright fame

Roberto

Bright fame

Robin

Bright fame

Rocco

Rest

Rocky

Formed of rock

Roderick

Famous ruler

Rodney

Fame/Acknowledged One

Rodolfo

Wolf

Rodrigo

Famous ruler

Rogan

Redhead

Roger

Famous spear

Rohan

Ascending

Roland

Famous land

Rolando

Famous land

Roman

From Rome

Rome

Capital City of Italy

Romeo

Pilgrim to Rome

Ronald

Advice

Ronan

Little seal

Ronin

Little seal

Rory

Redhead

Ross

Cliff

Rowan

Little redhead

Rowdy

Rowdy

Roy

Red

Rudy

Famous wolf

Russell

Little red one/ to make a noise

Ryan

Little king

Ryder

One who rides horseback

Ryker

Power

Rylan

Land of rye

Sage

Wisdom

Saïd

Master/ Lord

Salvador/ Sal/ Sally/ Sully (unisex)

Saviour

Salvatore

Saviour

Sami

Elevated

Samir

Pleasant companion

Samson

the Sun

Samuel/ Sam

God has heard

Sanjay

Victorious

Santiago

Saint James

Santino

He who is a Saint

Santos

the Holy Saints

Saul

He who was Prayed For

Sawyer

Woodcutter

Scott

Scotsman

Seamus

Supplanter/ He who supplies

Seán

God is gracious

Sebastian

From Sebaste

Seth

Appointed/ New Son (in Gnosticism and Ancient Judaism)

Shaan

Peaceful

Shane

God is gracious

Shaun

God is gracious

Shaurya

Valour

Shawn

God is gracious

Shea

Admirable

Sheldon

Valley with Steep Sides

Shepherd

One who guards sheep

Shia

God is my Own/ my Saviour

Shiloh

Tranquil

Shlomo

Peace

Siddharth

One who has accomplished a goal

Silas

Woods/ Forest

Simeon

He has heard

Simon

He has heard

Sincere

No Hypocrisy

Skyler

Scholar

Slade

Holy Valley

Smith

Blacksmith

Solomon

Peace-keeper

Sonny

A boy

Sören (pronounced S-u-r-u-n)

Stern

Spencer

Dispenser of provisions

Stanley

Stone clearing

Stefan

Crown

Stephen

Crown

Sterling

Excellent

Stetson

Son of Stephen

Steve

Crown

Steven

Crown

Stone

Stone

Stuart

Guardian of the house

Sullivan

Descendant of Súilleabháin

Sutton

South town/ town in Surrey, United Kingdom

Talan

Claw

Talon

Claw

Tanner

Tanner

Taylor

A tailor

Teagan

Descendent of Tadhgán

Teague

Poet

Ted

Rich guard

Teddy

Gift of god

Tejas

Texas

Terrell

To pull

Thatcher

Roof repairer

Theo

Gift of god

Theodore

Gift of god

Theron

Hunter

Thiago

Held by the heel

Thomas

Twin

Thor

Thunder

Tim

He who Honours God

Titan

Titan

Tobias

God is Good

Tobin

God is good

Toby

God is good

Todd

a small fox

Tom

Twin brother

Tomas

Twin

Tommy

Twin

Torin

Chief

Trace

Land belonging to Thracius

Tracy

Land belonging to Thracius

Trae

Three

Travis

Toll Collector

Tremaine

Rock settlement

Trent

He who lives by the River Trent

Trenton

Trent's town

Trever

Large village

Trevor

a large village

Trey

Three

Ulises

To hate

Umar

Thriving

Uri

My Light

Uriah

God is my light

Uriel

God is my light

Usher

To escort

Usman

Baby crane

Uziel

God is my power

Uzziah

God is my power

Valentin

Healthy/ Strong

Valentino

Healthy/ Strong

Vance

Marsh dweller

Varun

He who withholds

Vaughn

Little

Veer

Summer

Vernon

Land of alder trees

Vicente

Conquer

Victor

He who is victorious

Vidal

Life/ Livelihood/ Alive

Viggo

War

Vihaan

New light

Vince

Conquer

Vincent

Conquer

Vincenzo

Conquer

Vito

Life

Vladimir

Great ruler

Wade

Ford

Wallace

a Foreigner

Walter

Ruler of the army

Warren

Animal cage/ a community of wild rabbits

Waylon

War land

Wayne

Wagon maker

Wes

West meadow

Wesley

West meadow

Weston

West town

Wiley

Temple clearing

Will

Desire

Willem

Desired

William

Protection/ Helmet

Willie

Desire

Wilmer

Famous desire

Wilson

Son of William

Winston

Joy stone

Wyatt

Brave in war

Wylie

Temple clearing

Xaiver

New house

Xander

Defender of men

Xavi

New house

Yaakov

Supplanter

Yadiel

God is my fortune

Yael

Goat

Yahya

God is gracious

Yair

He will shine

Yakov

Supplanter

Yamil

Beautiful

Yariel

Lion of God

Yash

Fame

Yasir

He who will be rich

Yechiel

God lives

Yehoshua

(the Aramaic name of Jesus) God is salvation

Yehuda

Gratitude

Yisroel

God contended

Yitzchok

He laughs

Yoel

God is Lord

Yonatan

Given by God

Yoni

Given by God

Yosef

God increases

Yousef

boy God increases

Yovani

God is gracious

Yuki

Snow (Japanese Origin)

Yusuf

God increases

Zachariah

The Lord remembers You

Zachary

The Lord remembers

Zachery

God remembers

Zack

God remembers

Zackary

God remembers

Zade

Ever Increasing

Zaid

Ever Increasing

Zain

His Majestic Beauty

Zakaria

May God remember

Zander

Defender of men

Zavier

New house

Zeke

God will give you strength

Zephaniah

God has hidden

Zephyr

West wind

Zev

Wolf

Zion

Jerusalem

Zyair

River that swallows all rivers

Zyaire

River that swallows all rivers

POPULAR NAMES BY YEAR

(2016-2019)

We understand that trends change and if you like to keep up to date with what's popular and in fashion, we don't blame you. Let's take a look at the most popular names for boys from 2016 to 2019.

2016

Jackson

Henry

Aiden

Kyle

Lucas

Liam

Noah

Ethan

Mason

Caden

Oliver

Elijah

Grayson

Jacob

Michael

Benjamin

Carter

James

Jayden

Logan

Alexander

Caleb

2017

Jake

Karl

Todd

Michael

Scott

Chad

Caleb

Jay

Jayden

Jon

Ben

Adam

Skyler

Stryker

Flynn

2018

Jackson

Jonah

Angelo

Mohammad

Ezra

Liam

Noah

Aiden

Caden

Grayson

Lucas

Mason

Oliver

Elijah

Zack

Paul

2019

George

Ollie

Leo

Arthur

Jack

Theo

Alfie

Oscar

Muhammed

Noah

Thomas

Joshua

Ethan

Jackson

Wyatt

Owen

Luke

Lucas

Gabriel Josiah

Matthew

Asher

FREQUENTLY ASKED QUESTIONS

Here are some of the most asked questions from parents who are in the process of choosing a name for their baby.

1. My partner and I disagree with names, what do we do?

This scenario is extremely common. You and your partner are different people with different opinions. Baby names are like flavours of ice cream. Everyone is different. The best situation is if you both compromise and find middle ground.

In order to do this, sit your partner down and you should both write a list of three names which you like. When you've done this, hand your list to your partner and take theirs. You both have to cross out two names. The name that remains on both lists will be your final two names.

From there, you both have to have a conversation about the name choice. Come to a mutual decision. If you still can't come to an understanding because one of you is not okay with the names they chose, then sit down with this book and go through names again. There is bound to be at least one name you can both agree on.

2. Is it okay to choose a feminine name for my son?

Absolutely! You're the parent and you decide. I've met many Leslies who are men and many Joes who are women. Of course you have to consider the social impact doing this will have on your baby. While there is nothing wrong with naming your son '*Emily*', be aware of the impact that will have on your son's life. While it sounds harsh, many kids who are named unisex and opposite sex names are more likely to be taunted or bullied at school.

3. Can I make up/invent a name for my baby?

Yes. Again, you have to be very careful with how you go about this. Making up a name based on another name is 100% fine but naming a child a word which out of context would be misinterpreted is not a good idea. Here are some examples of what is appropriate and what is not. The following are real names which people have named their babies.

Appropriate:

- Fox
- Leather
- Woolf
- Meclan

Inappropriate:

- Bus
- Cup
- Tea-Leaf
- Tackle

You have to make the responsible decision if you have a name in mind which isn't usual.

4. Can I use an alternate spelling for my baby's name?

Of course. In fact, this is encouraged in a lot of cases because alternate spellings can make for some of the most original and beautiful names in the world. For example:

- Adrienn instead of Adrien
- Melisha instead of Melissa
- Franceen instead of Francine
- Lili instead of Lily

Once more, responsibility is key. Not going overboard is a principal aspect of using alternate spellings for baby names.

5. Can I call my baby a name from a different culture to my own?

Can you? Yes.

Should you? It depends.

There are times when doing this could be misconstrued as offensive if you aren't 100% sure of the meaning of a name in another language. In 2012, a man famously made it onto the local newspapers in the South of England because he named his daughter a Chinese name without properly researching the etymology and meaning of the name. It turns out he called her 'Loud Peanut' which is funny but unfortunate.

If you admire a certain culture or language and do the right research behind an ethnic/cultural name, then it would be a lovely tribute to name your child in that language.

6. Can I name my child after myself?

Yes. This is actually called 'juniorising'. Juniorising is where you name your child after his/her father or mother. The name 'jr' (abbreviation of 'junior') follows after his/her name to show this.

Printed in Great Britain
by Amazon